When I photograph, I search for the weird and out of place. In The States, I find this task challenging, and fulfilling; we have standardized our land and are desensitized to what we see everyday. In Cuba, I found this to be the opposite. The weird and out of place were right in front of me and existed as part of the environment. I deemed Cuba a "displaced place," and I believe that is due to its untouched quality. I found myself incredibly lucky to visit Cuba at such a crucial time, before our American influence becomes their new-formed identity. These photographs convey my view of Cuba, in all its quirkiness.

Brooke Goldman

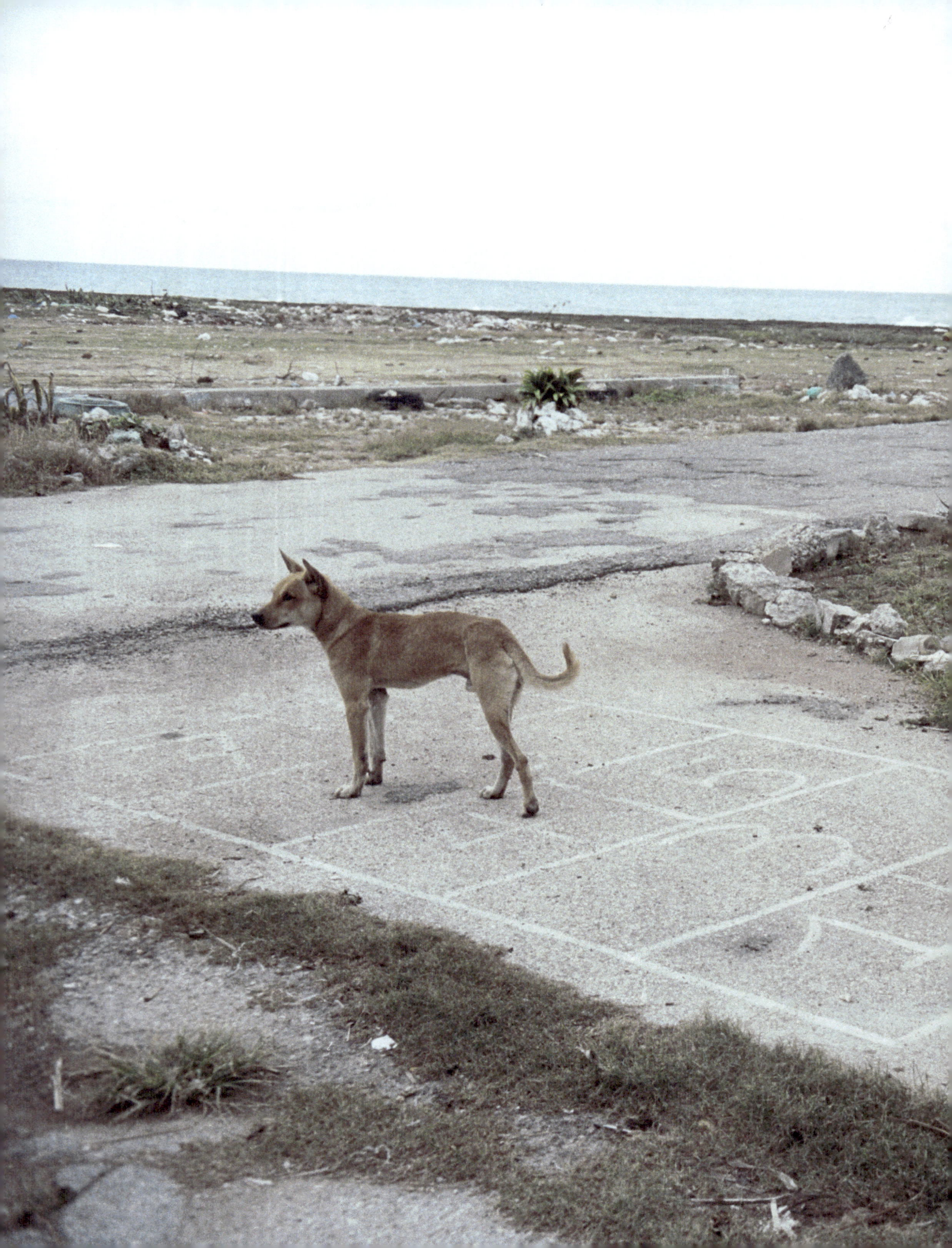

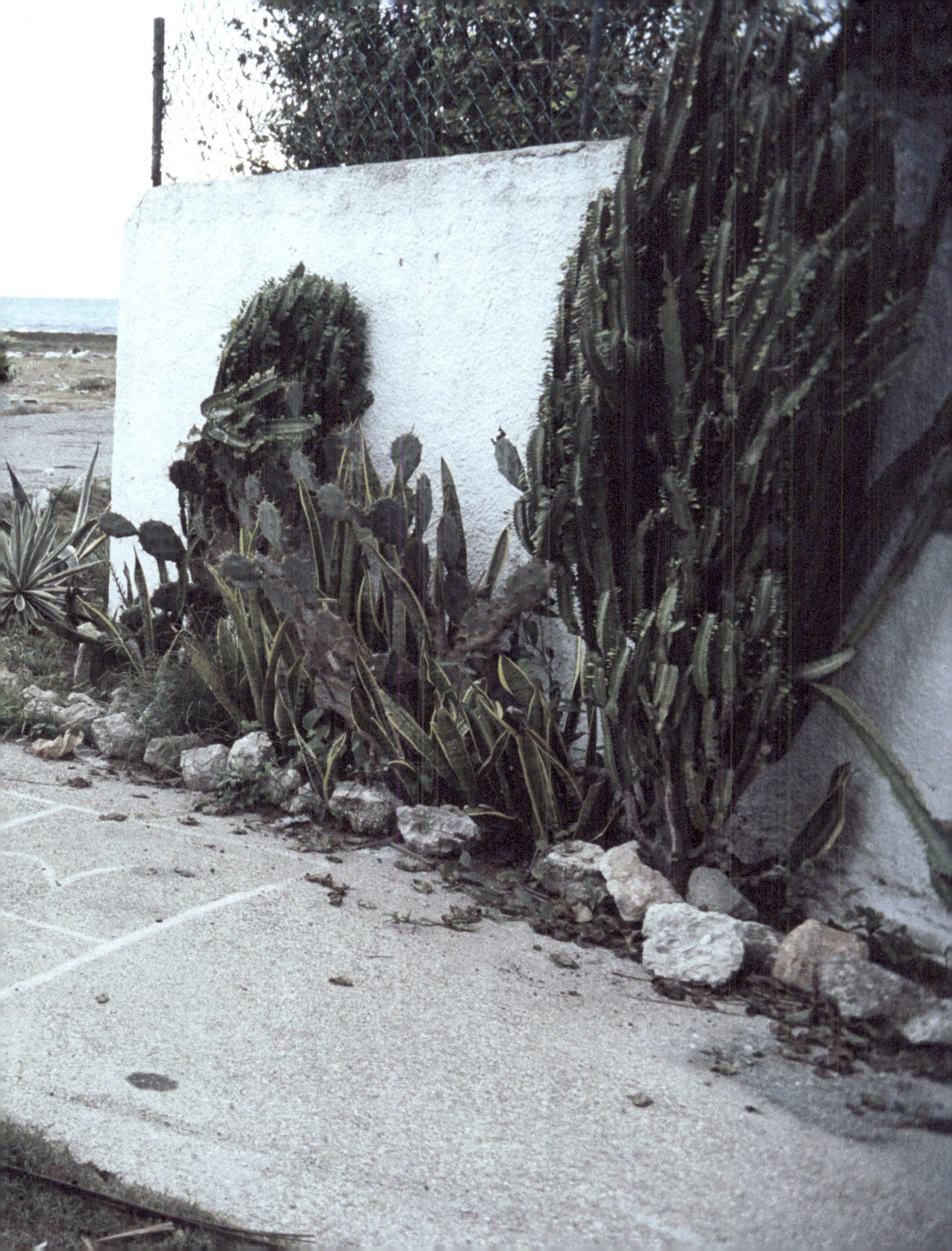

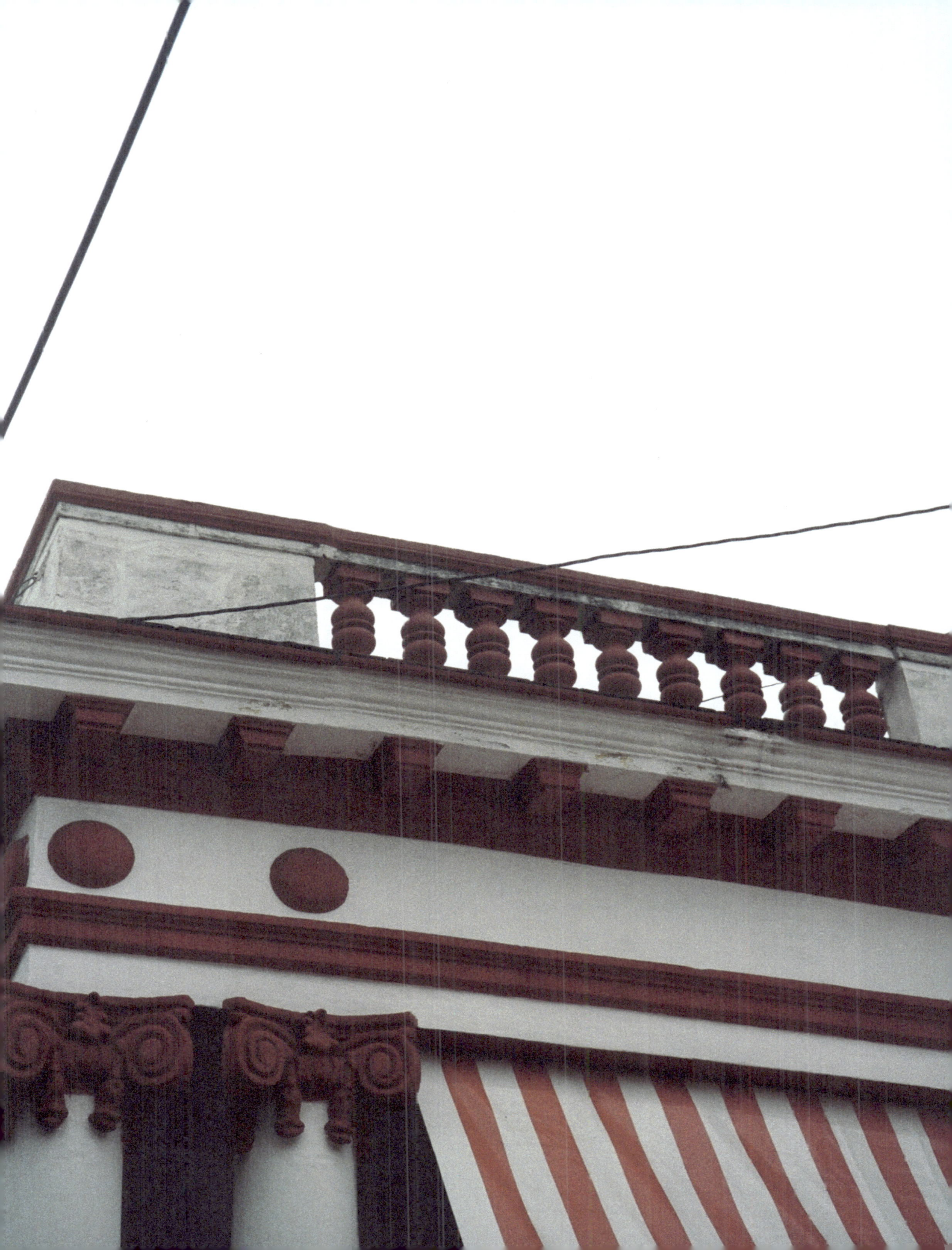

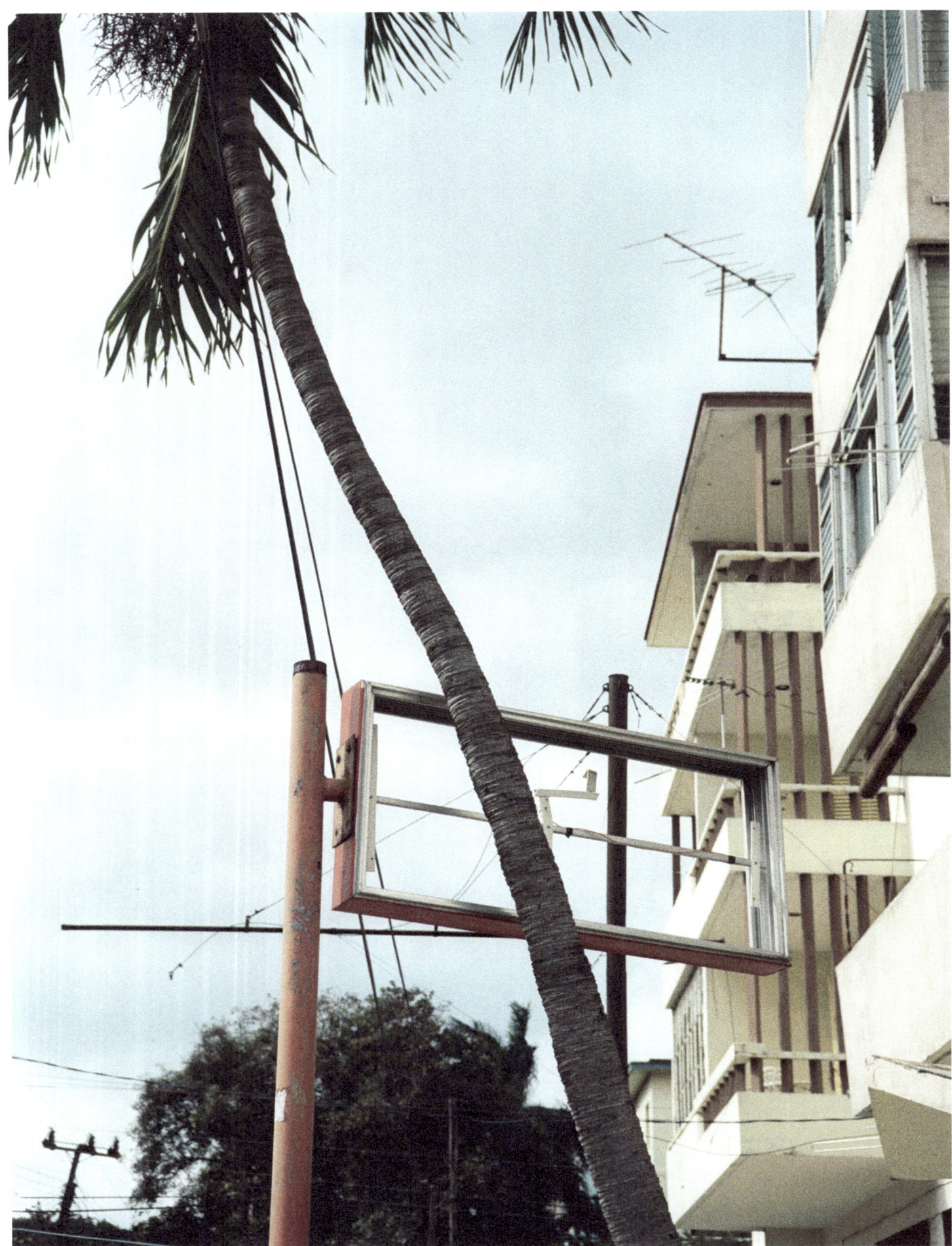

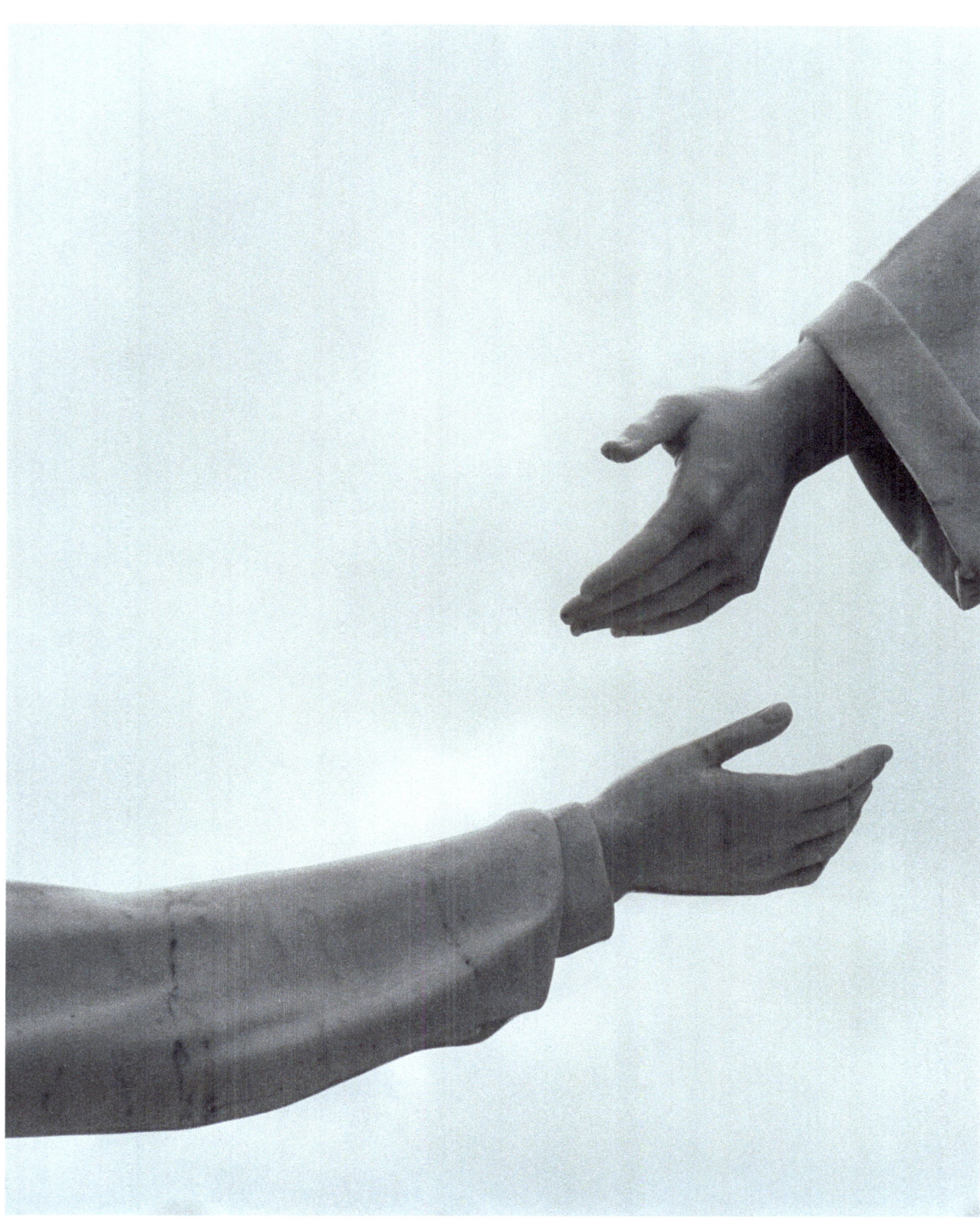

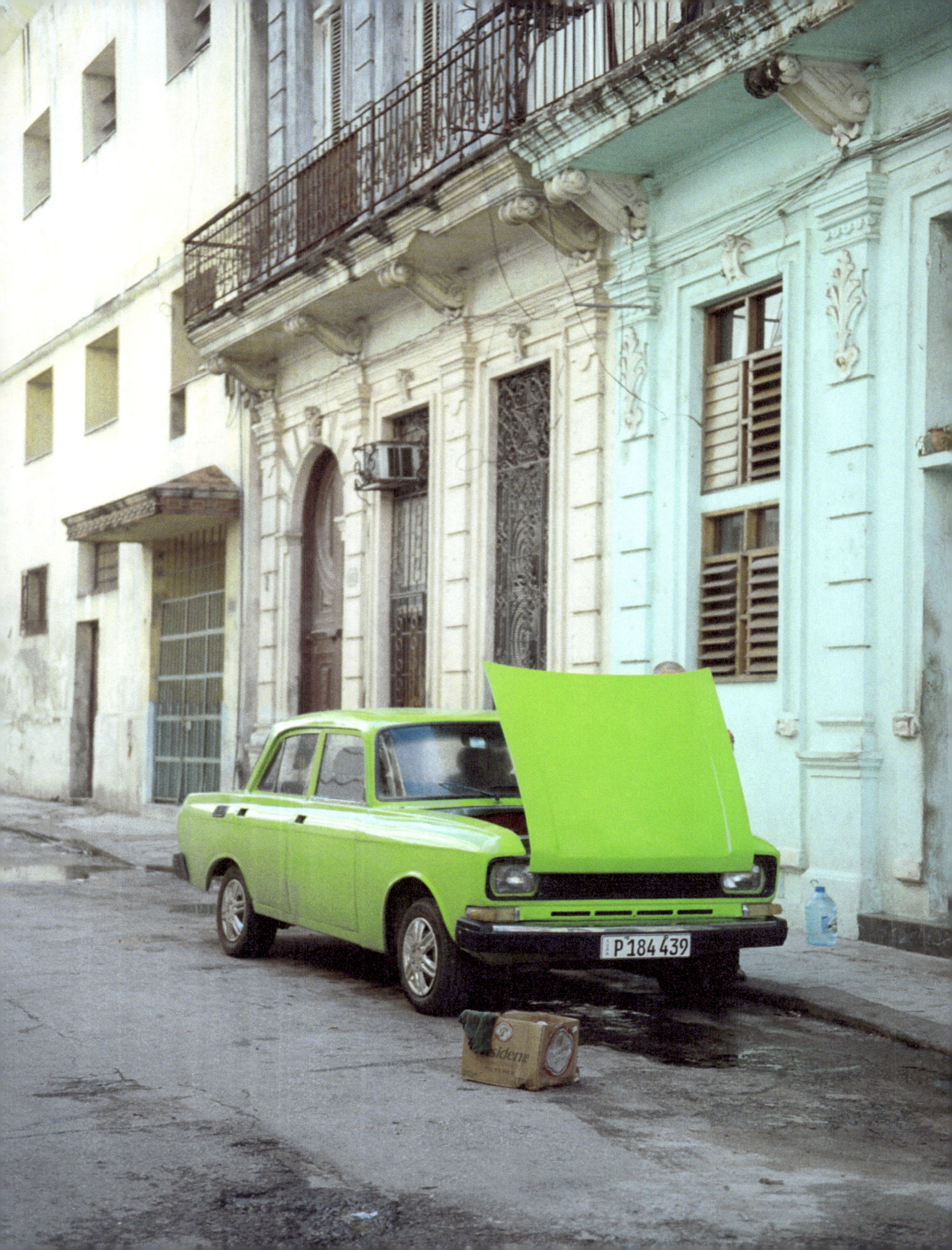

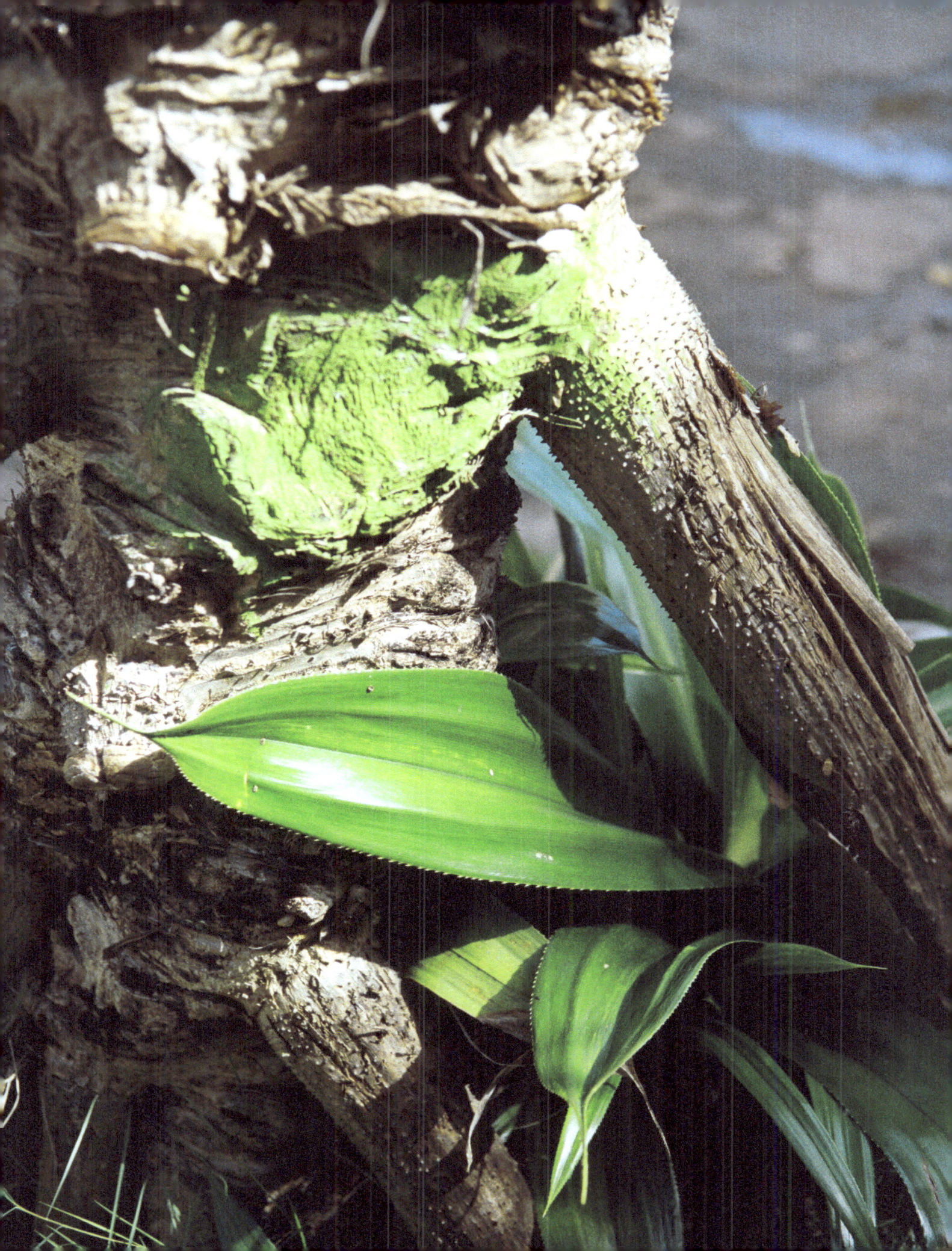

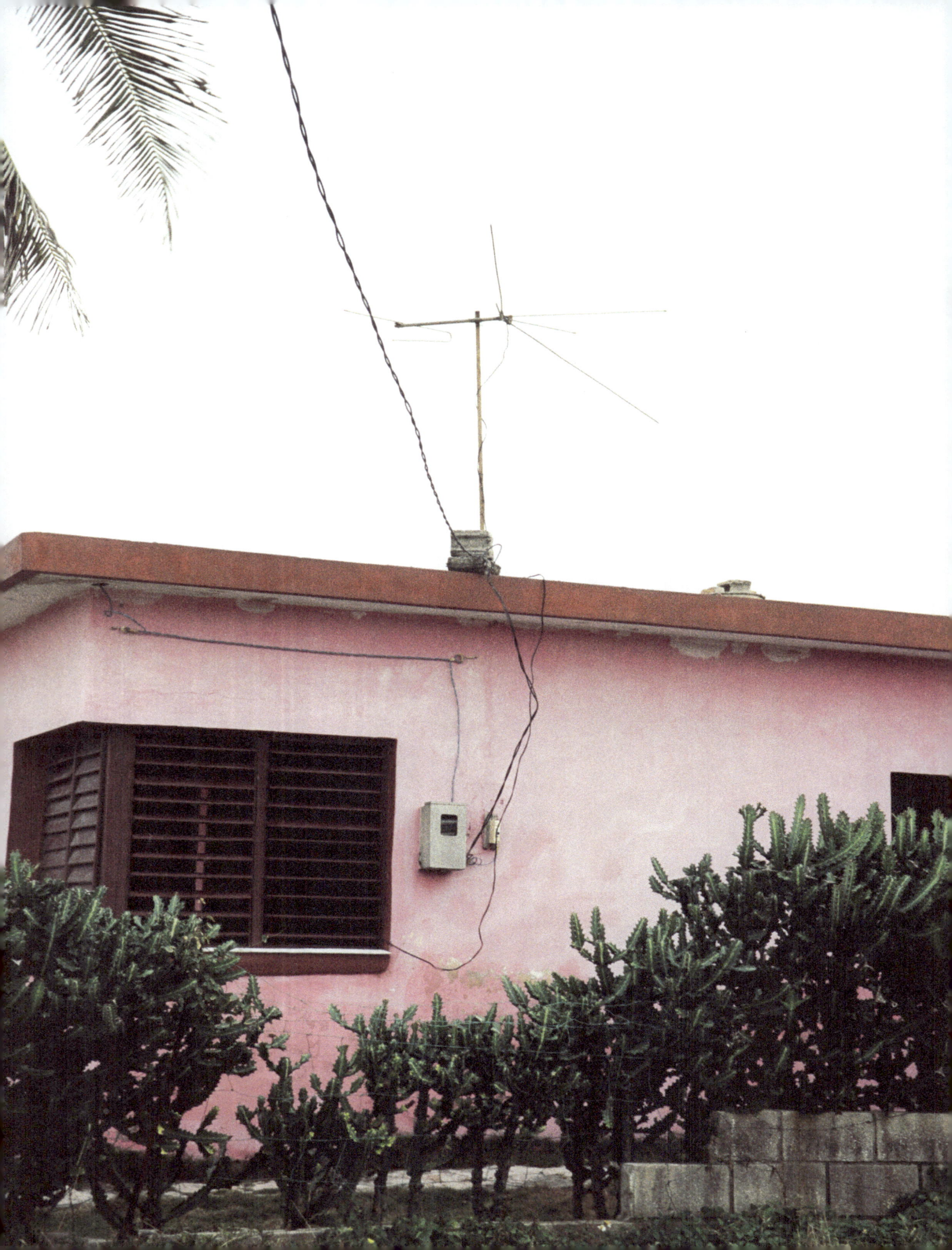

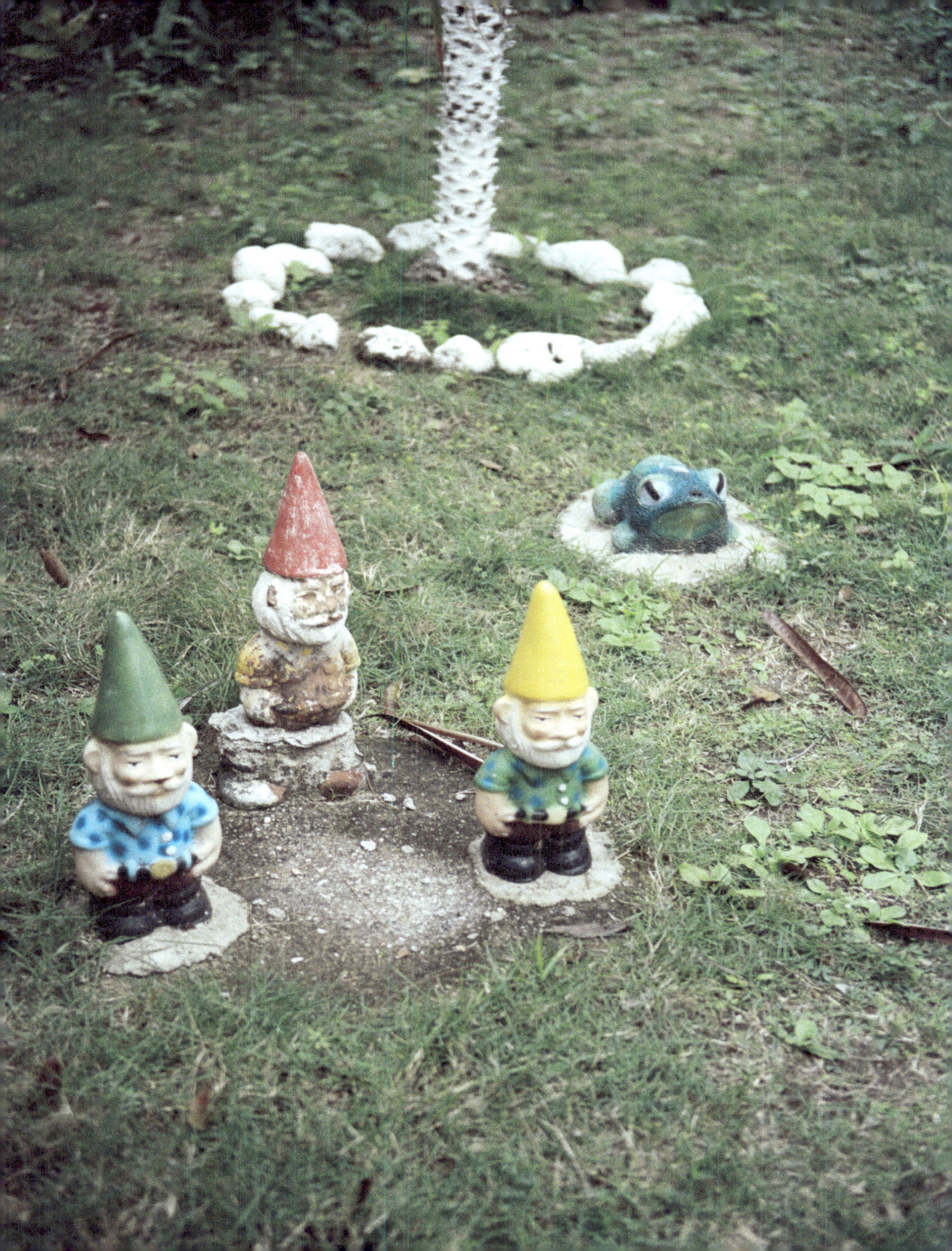

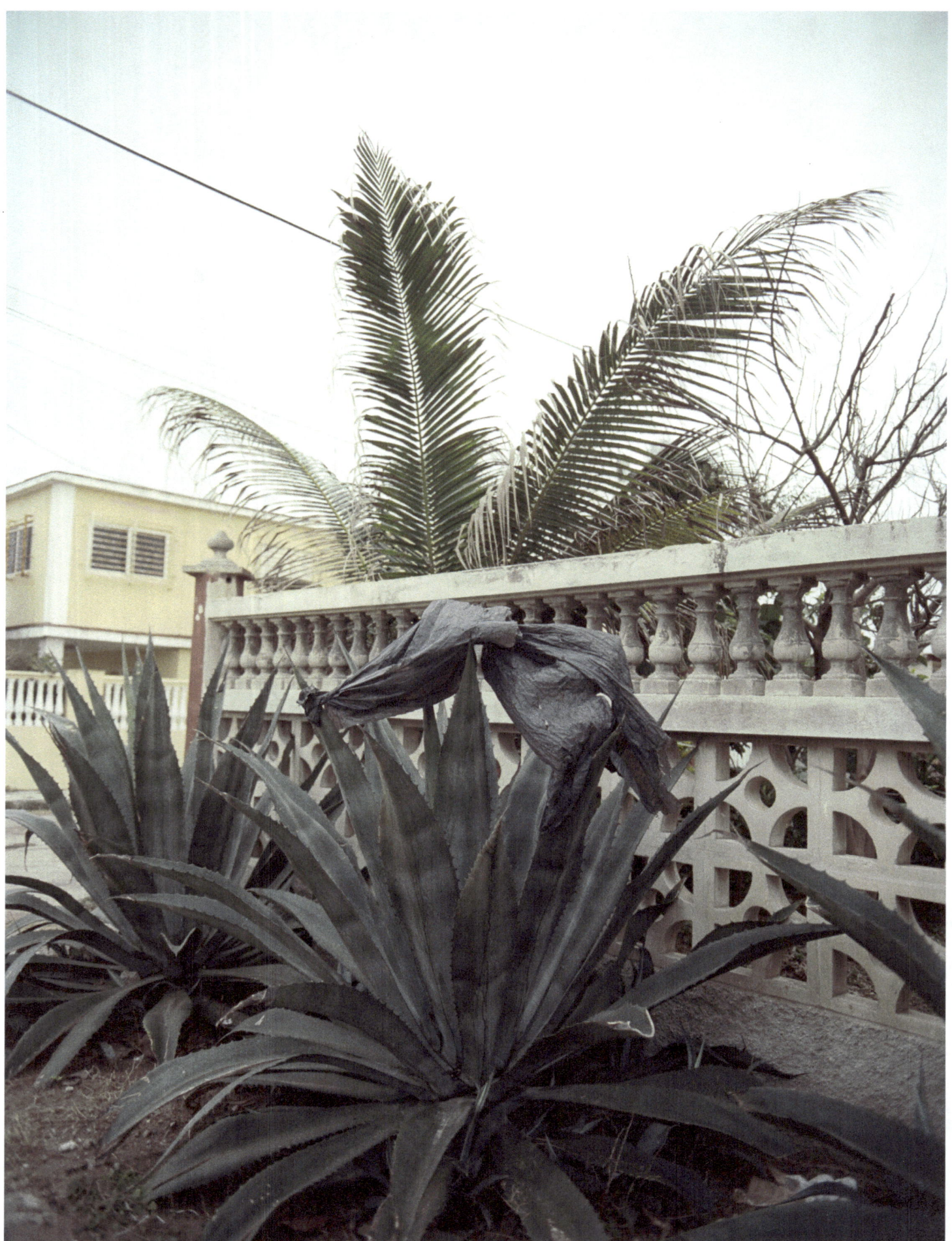

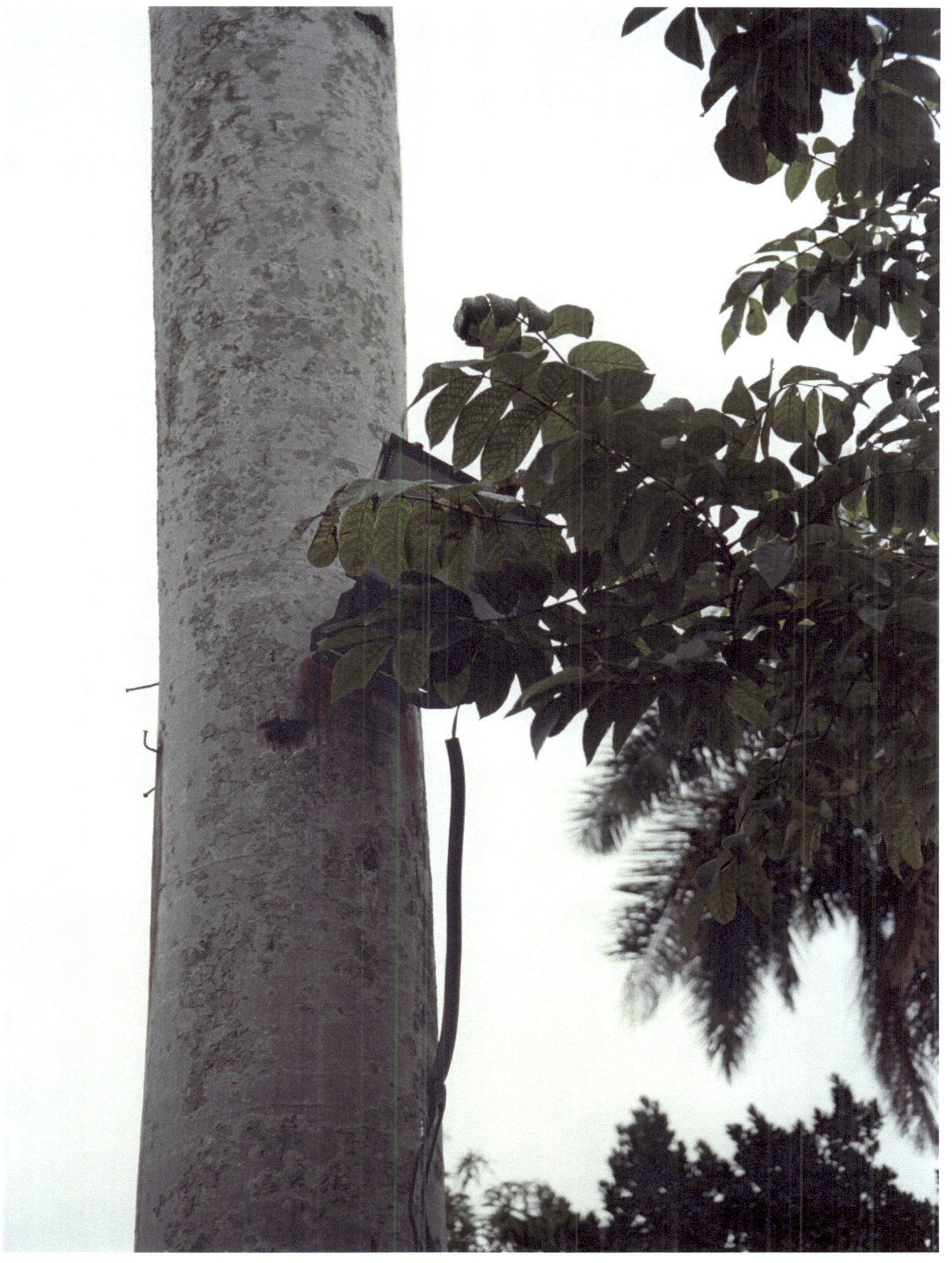

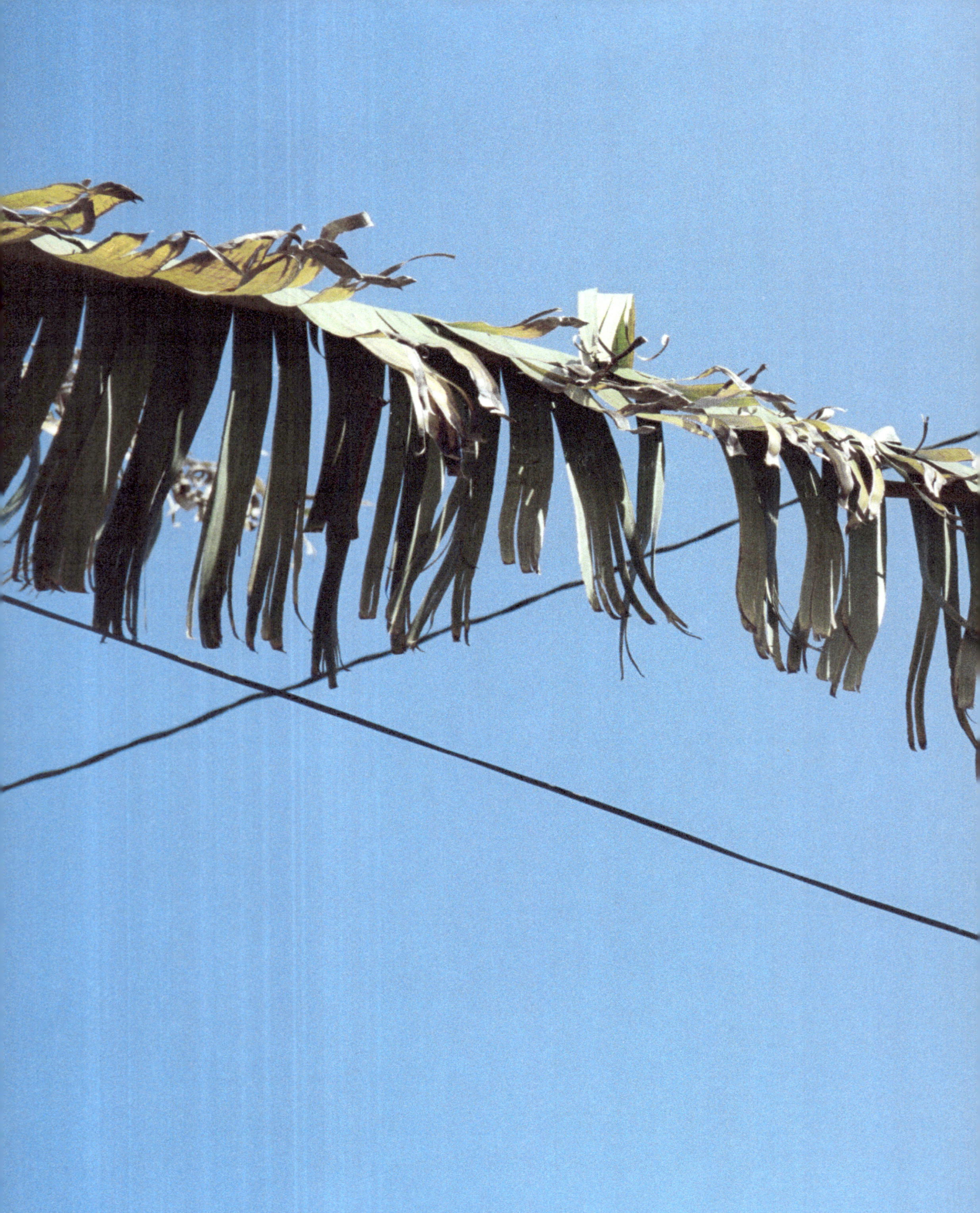

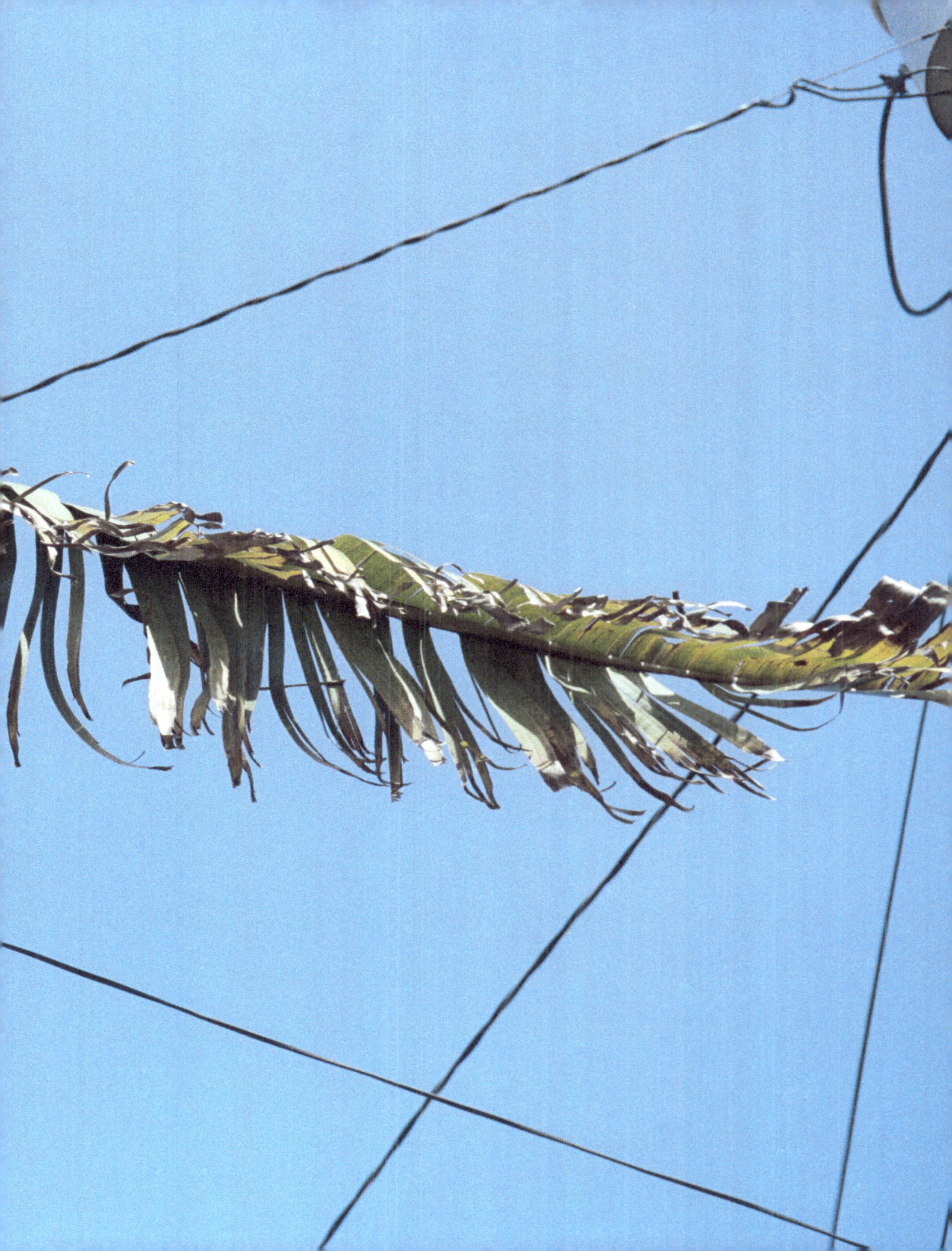

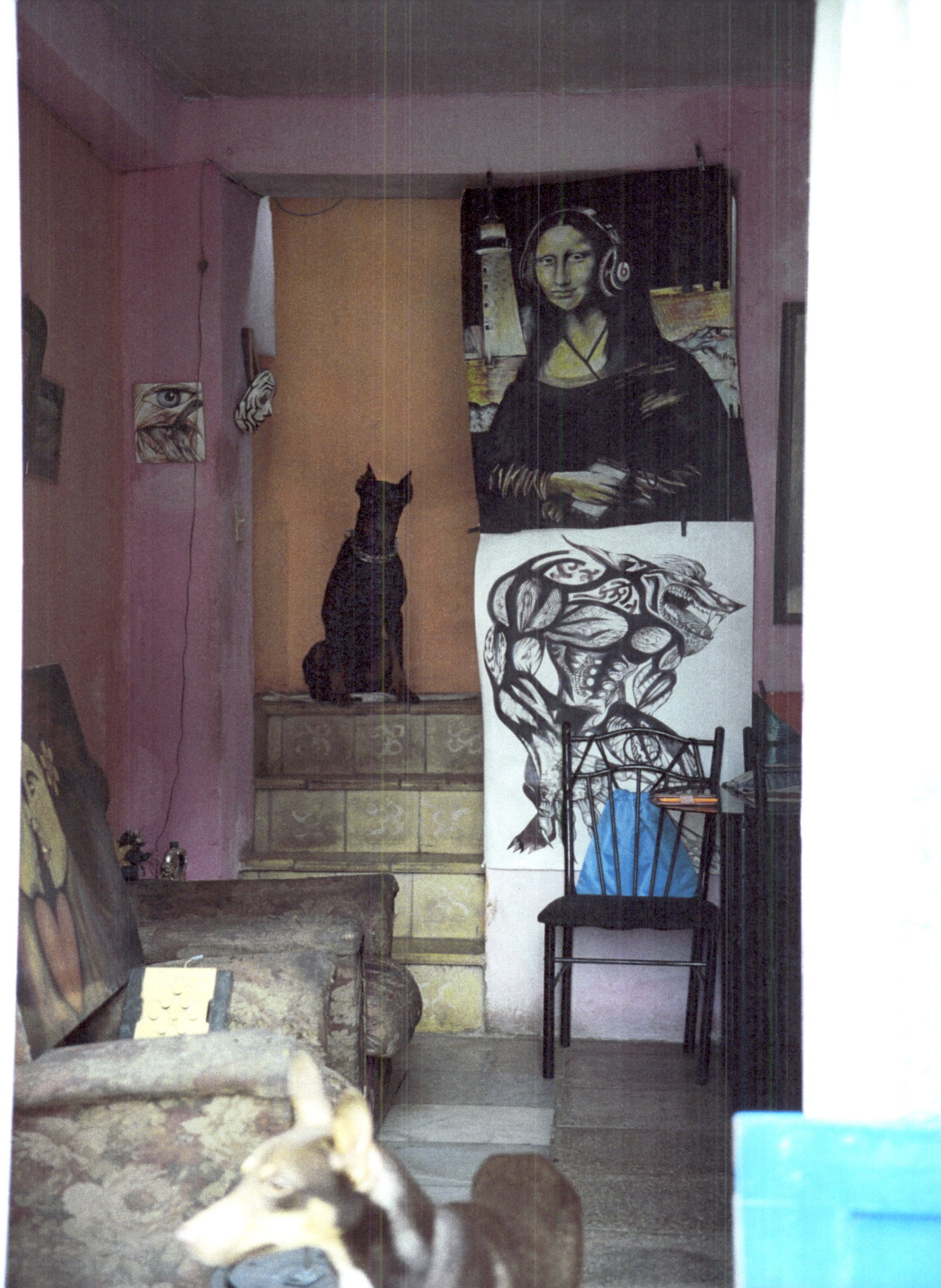

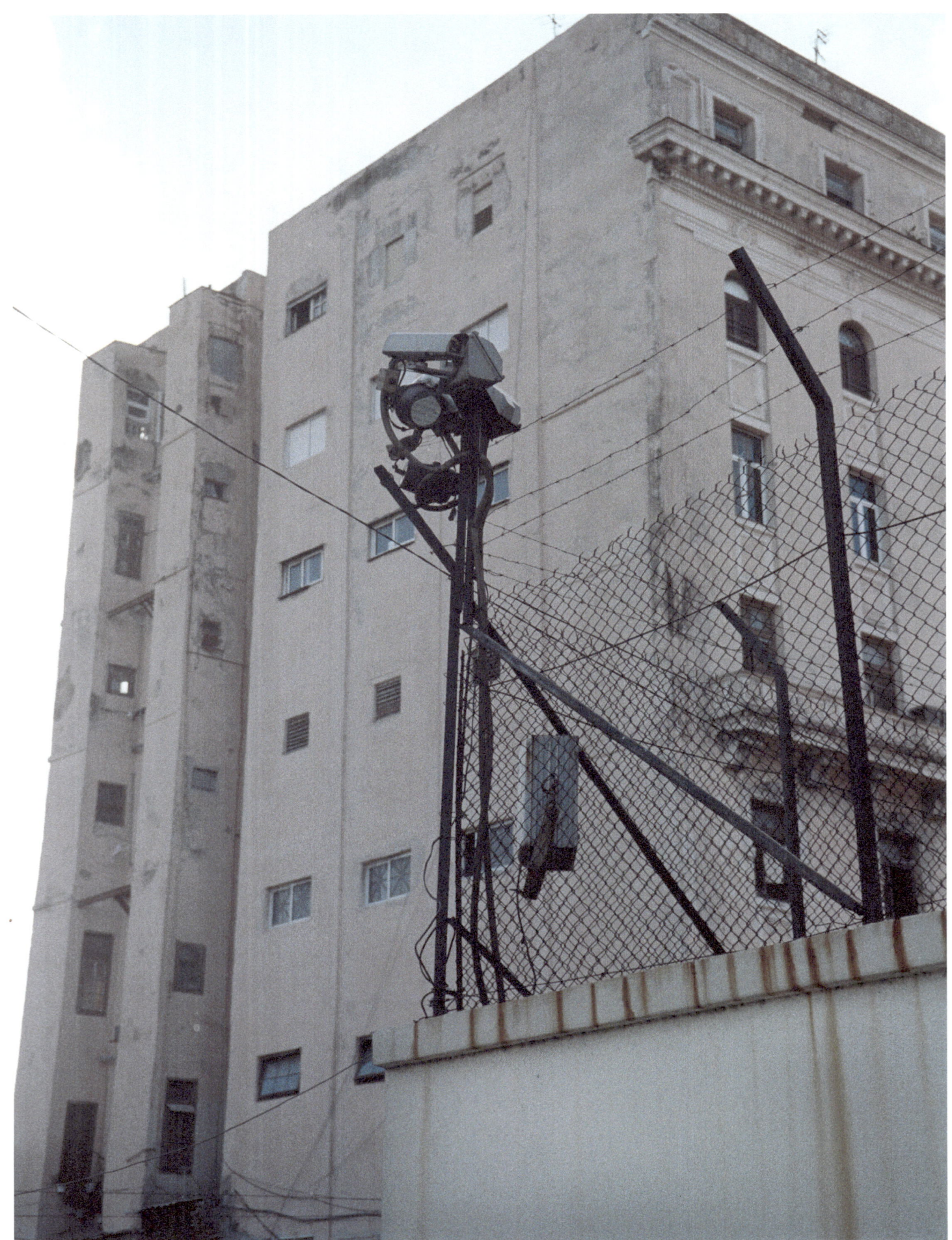

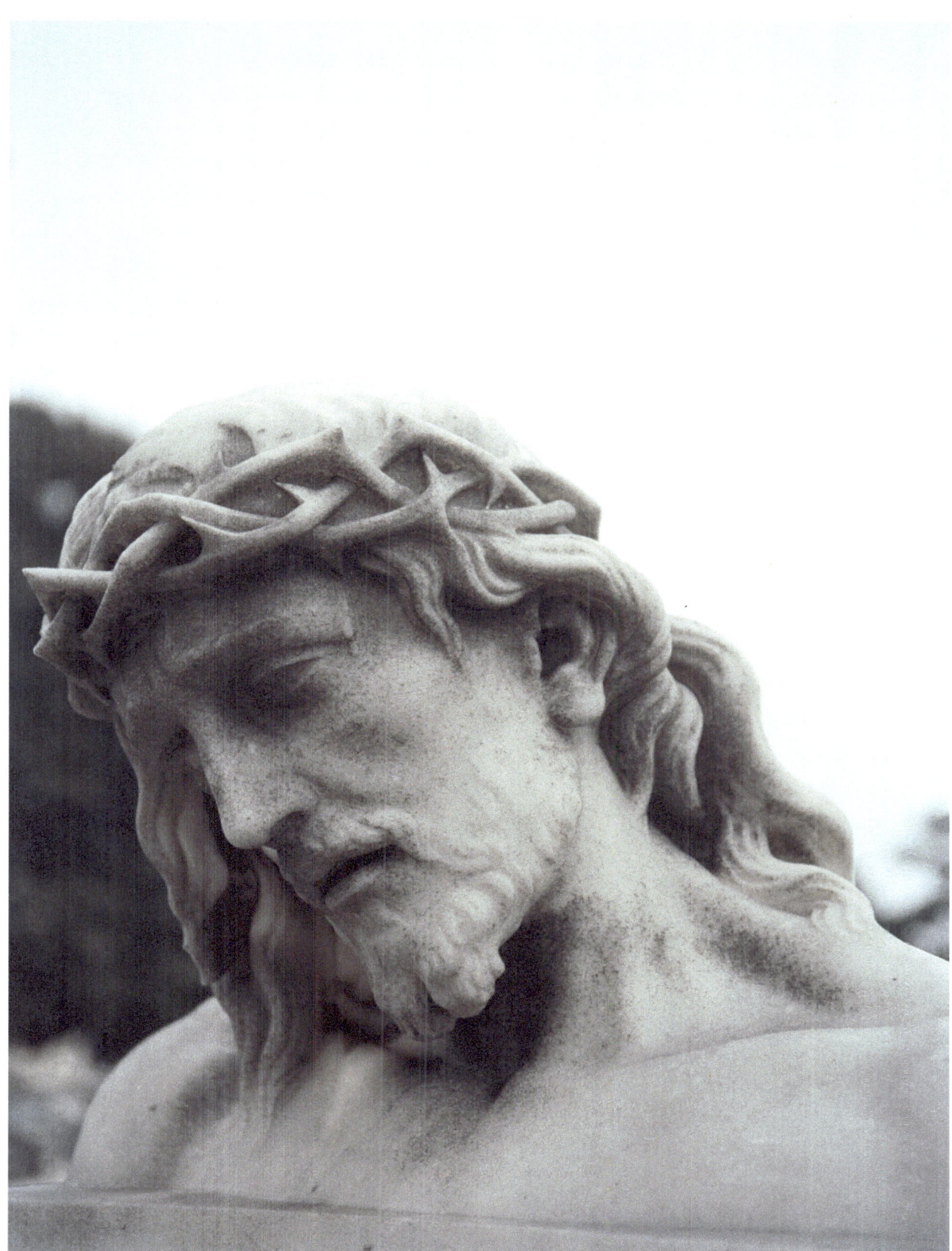

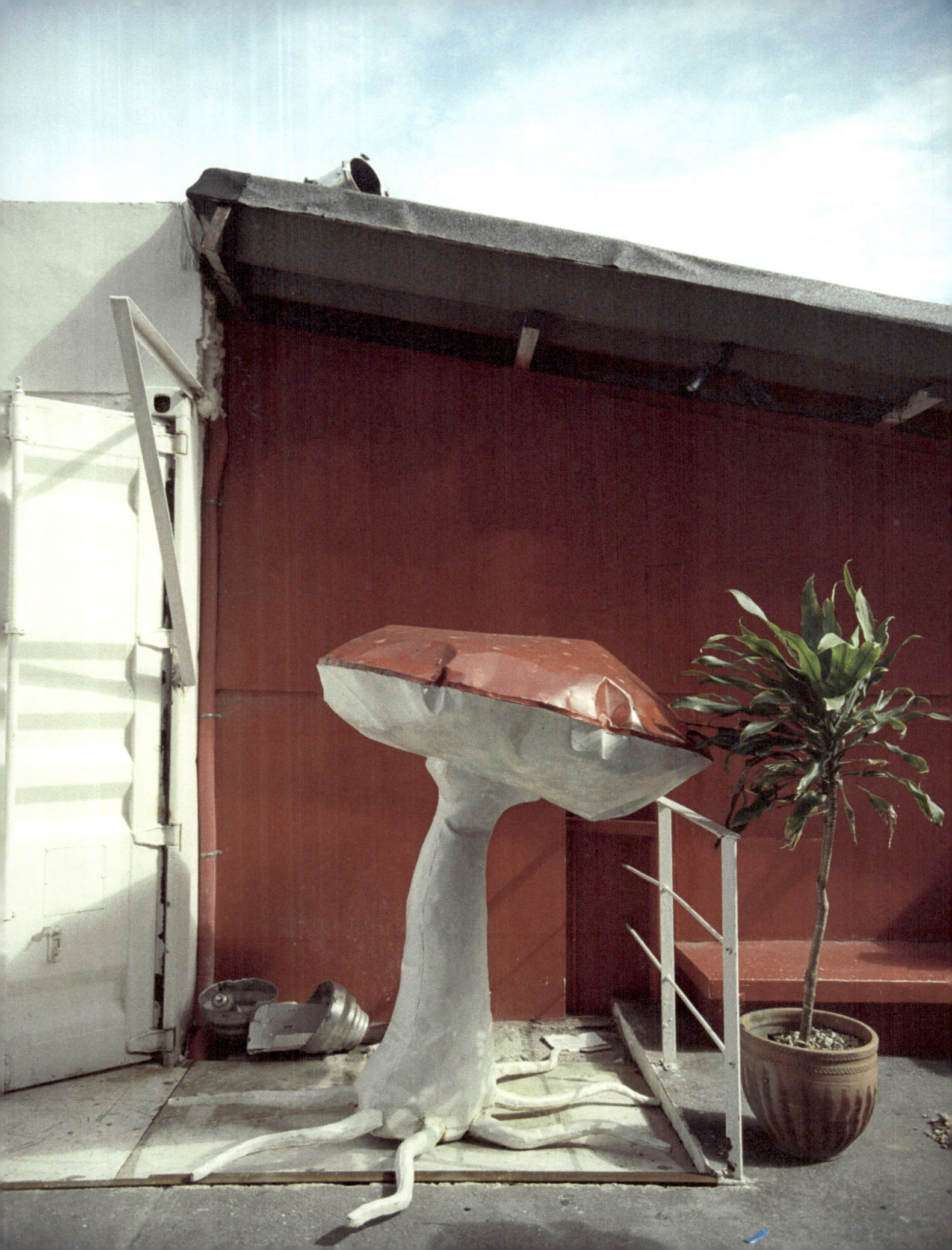

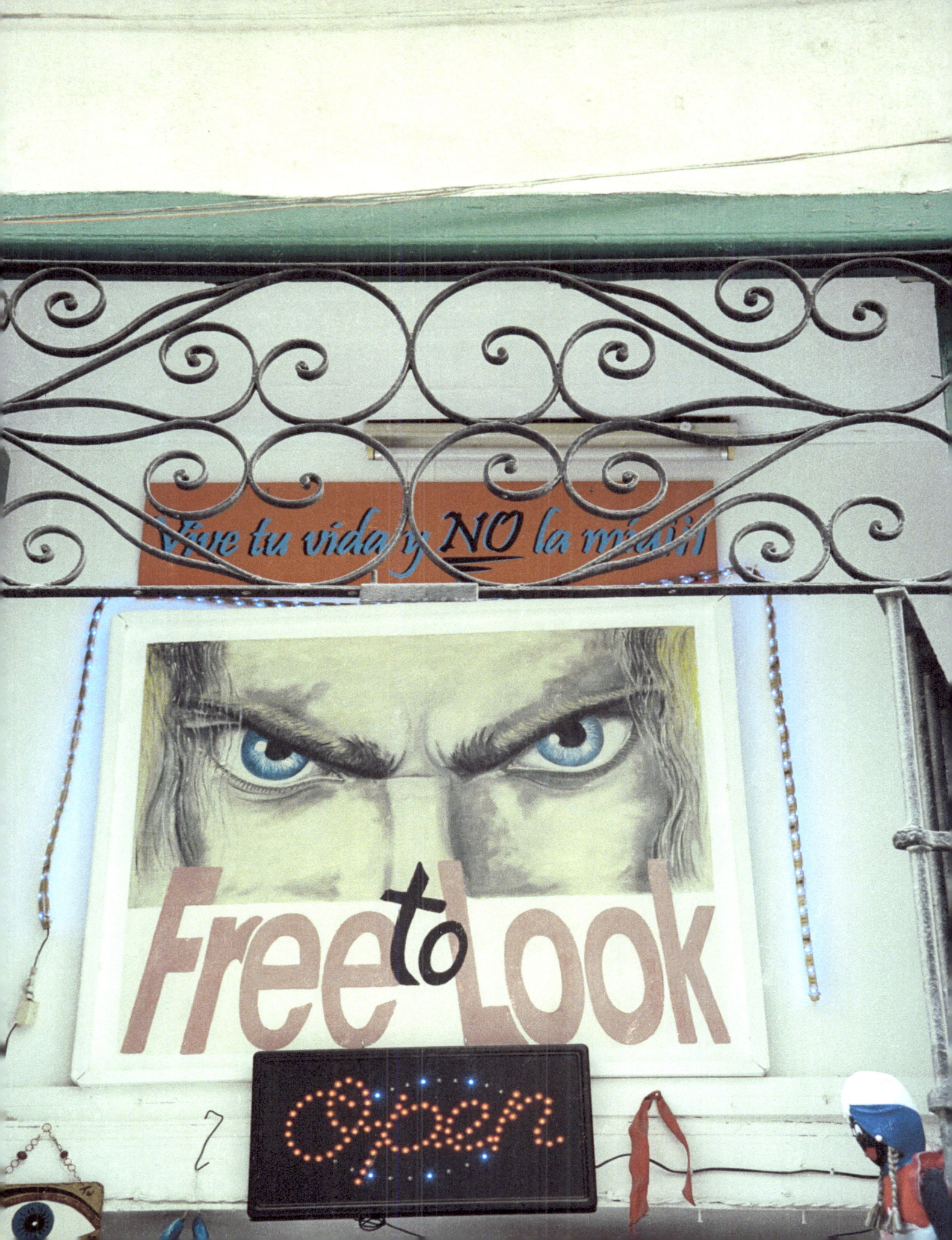

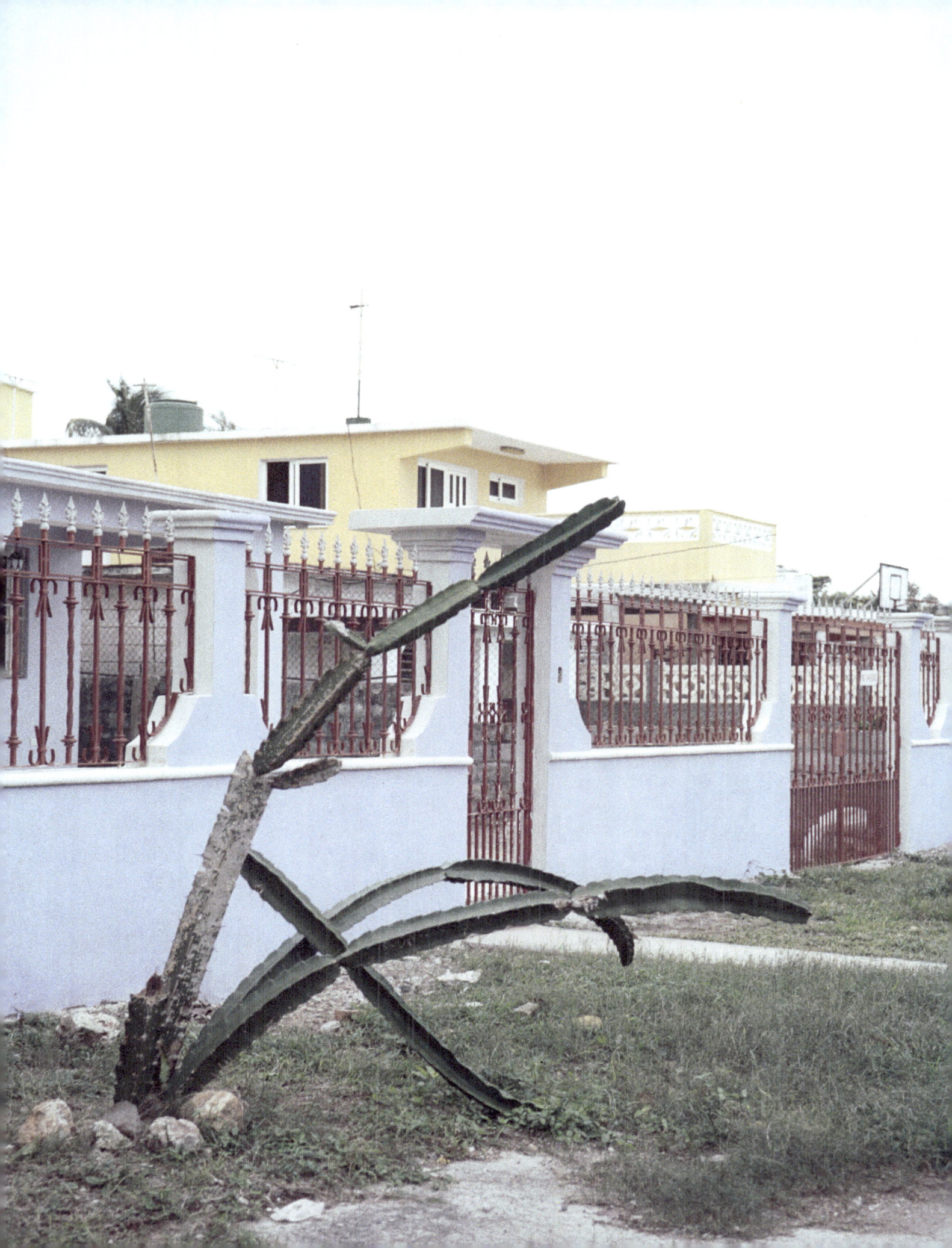

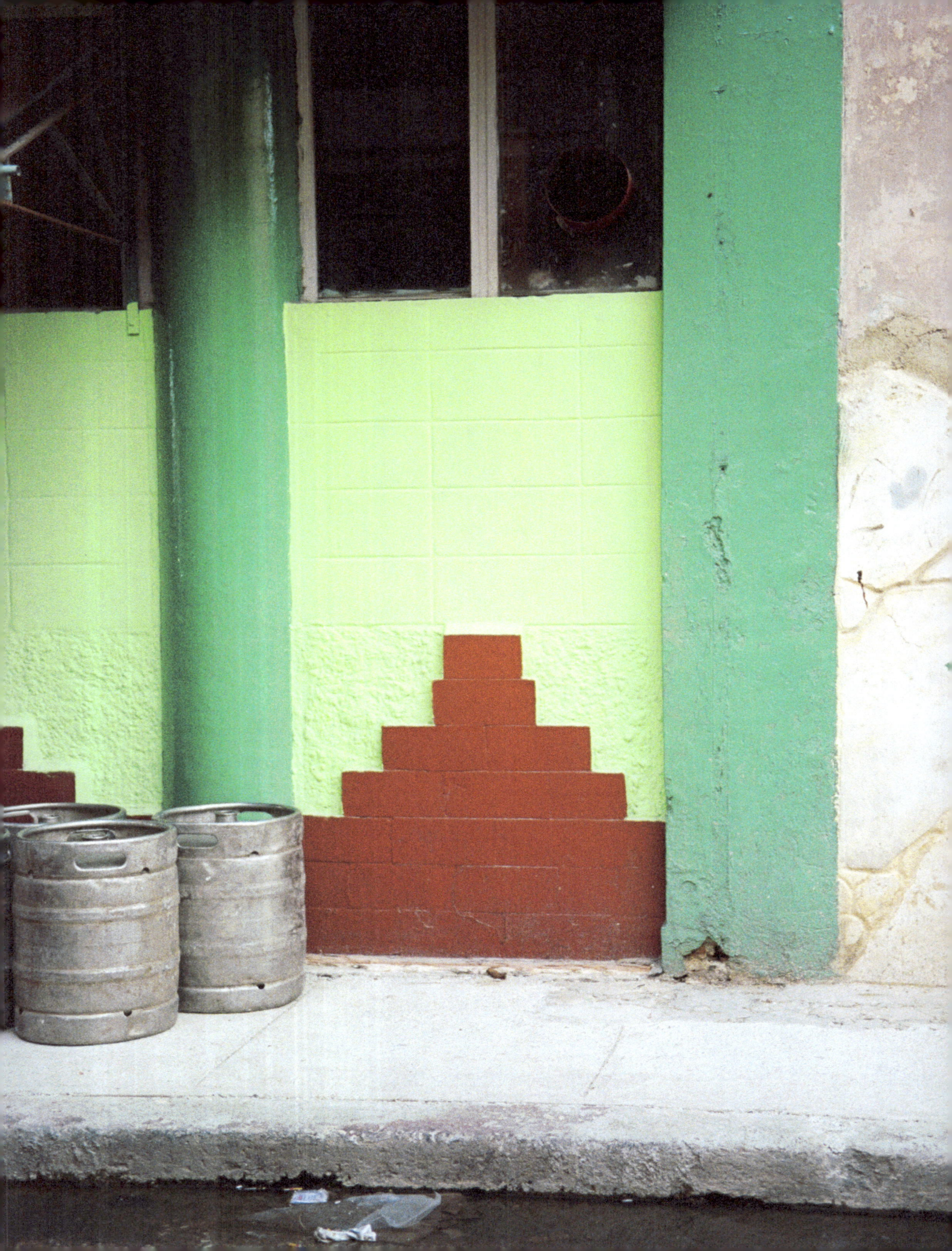

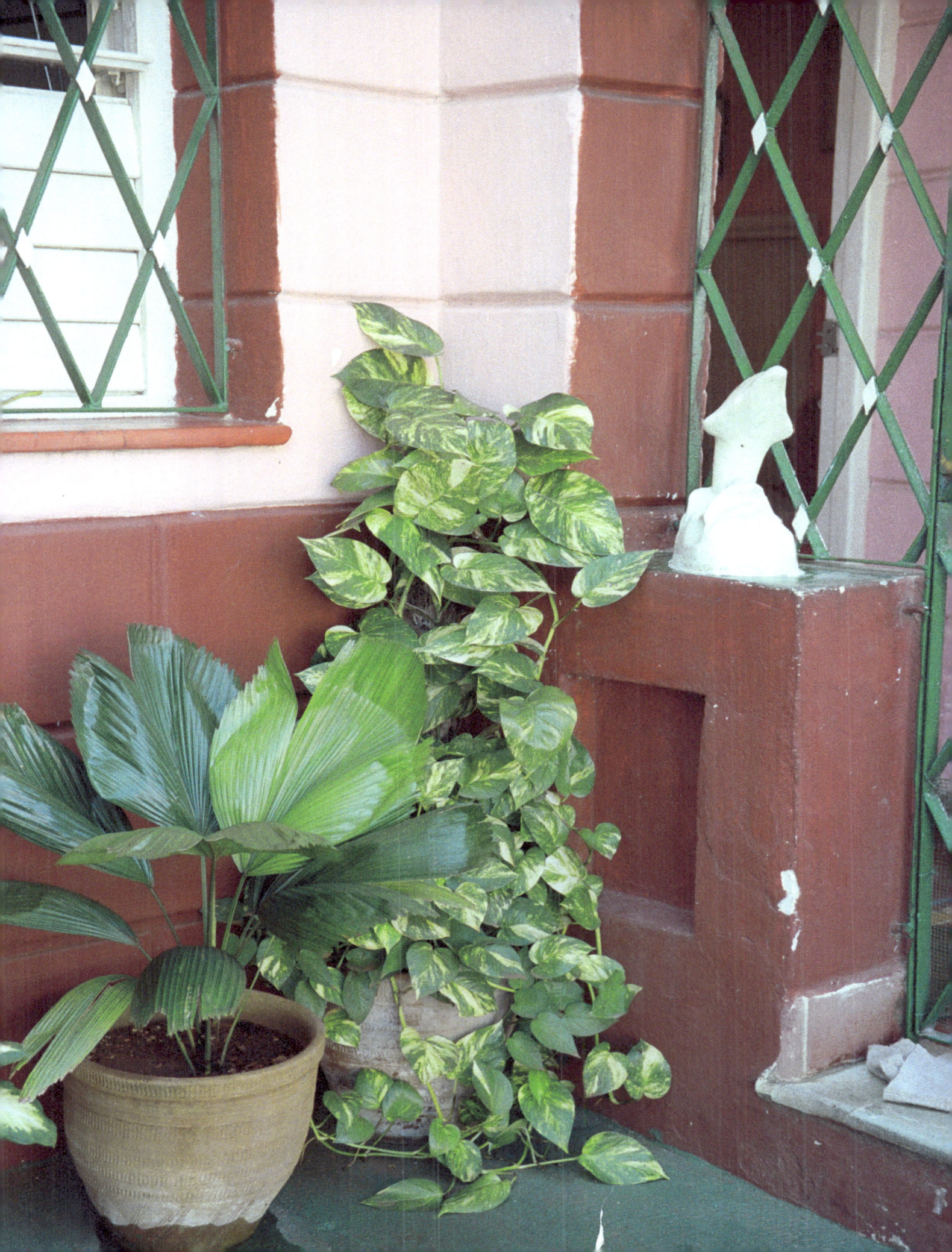

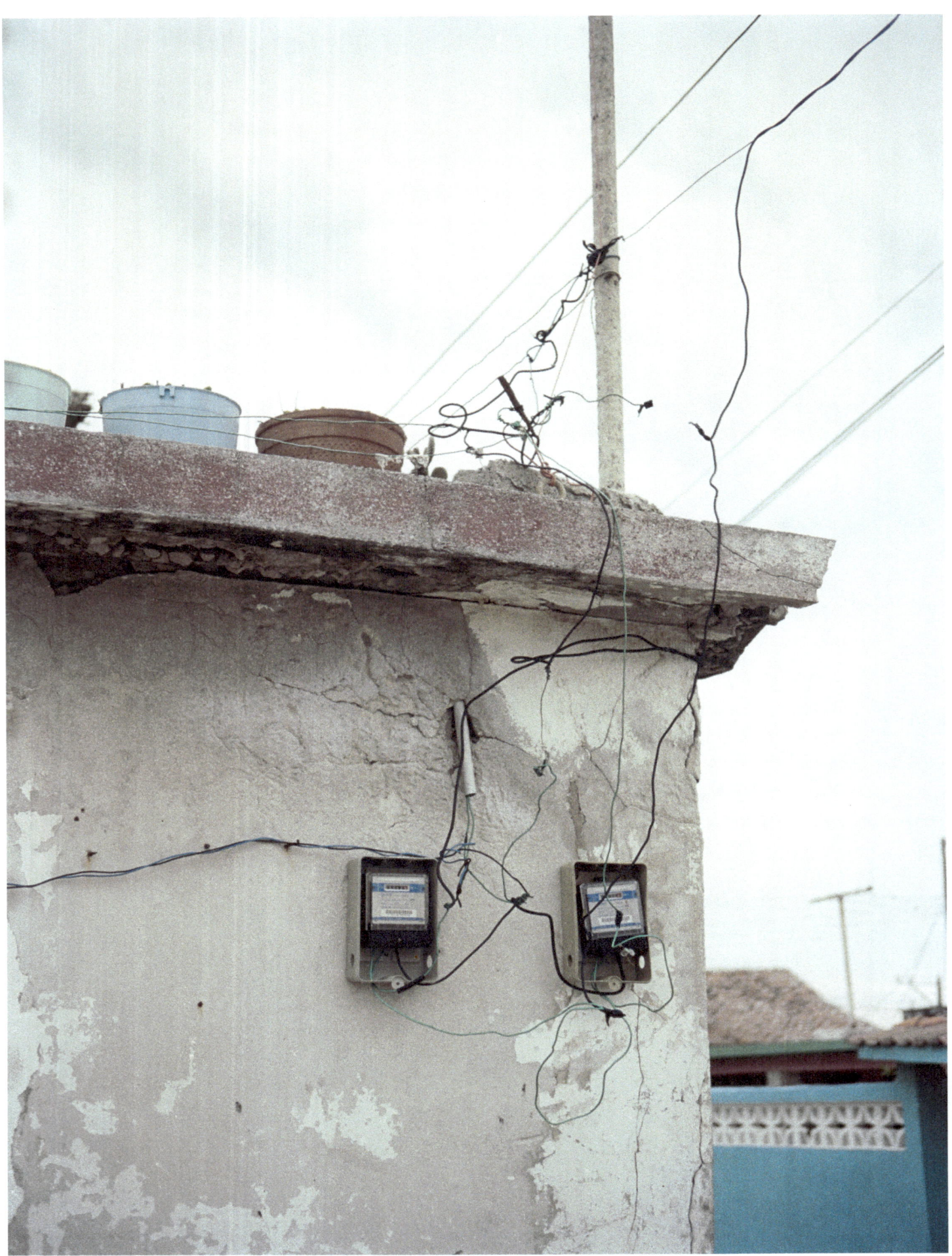

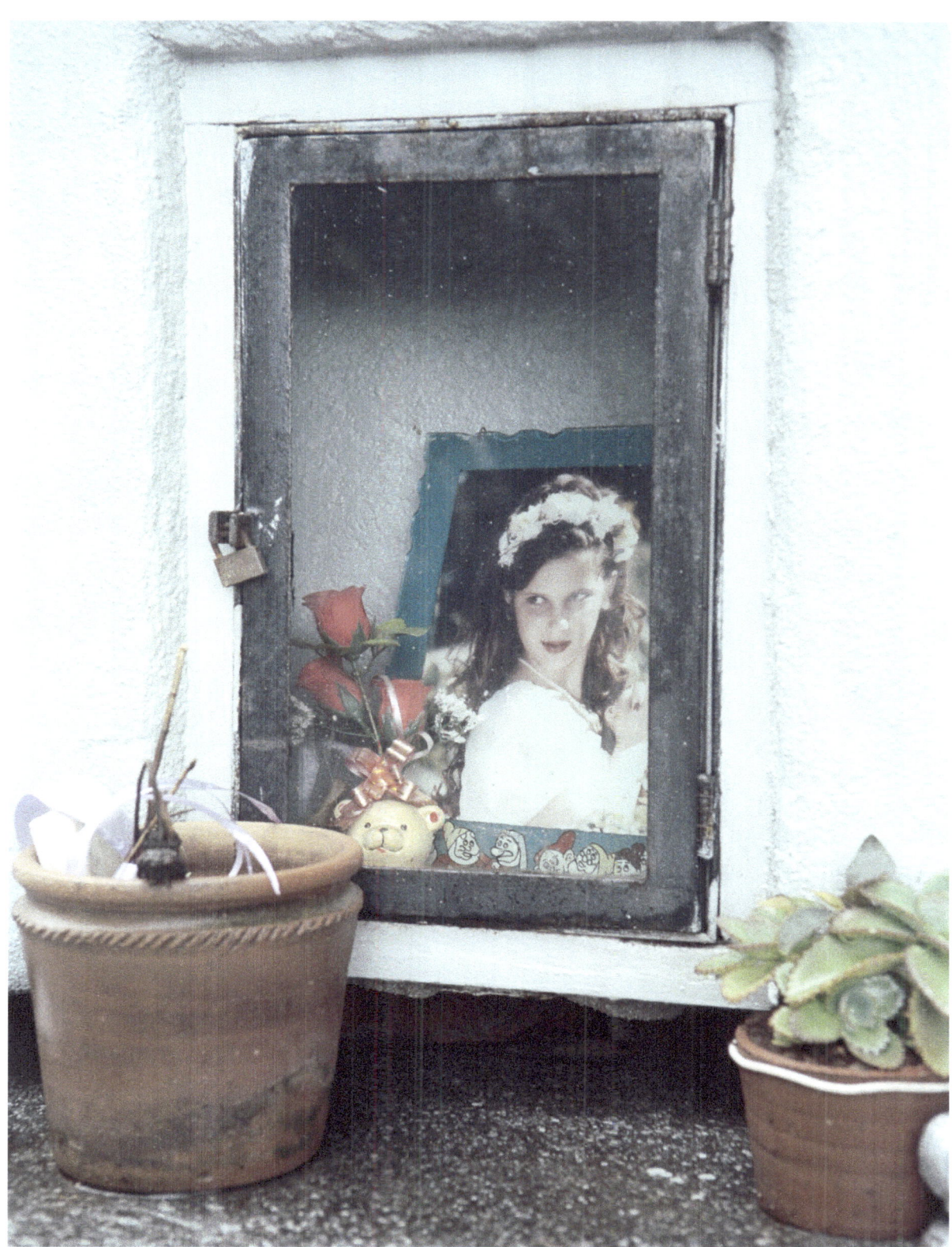

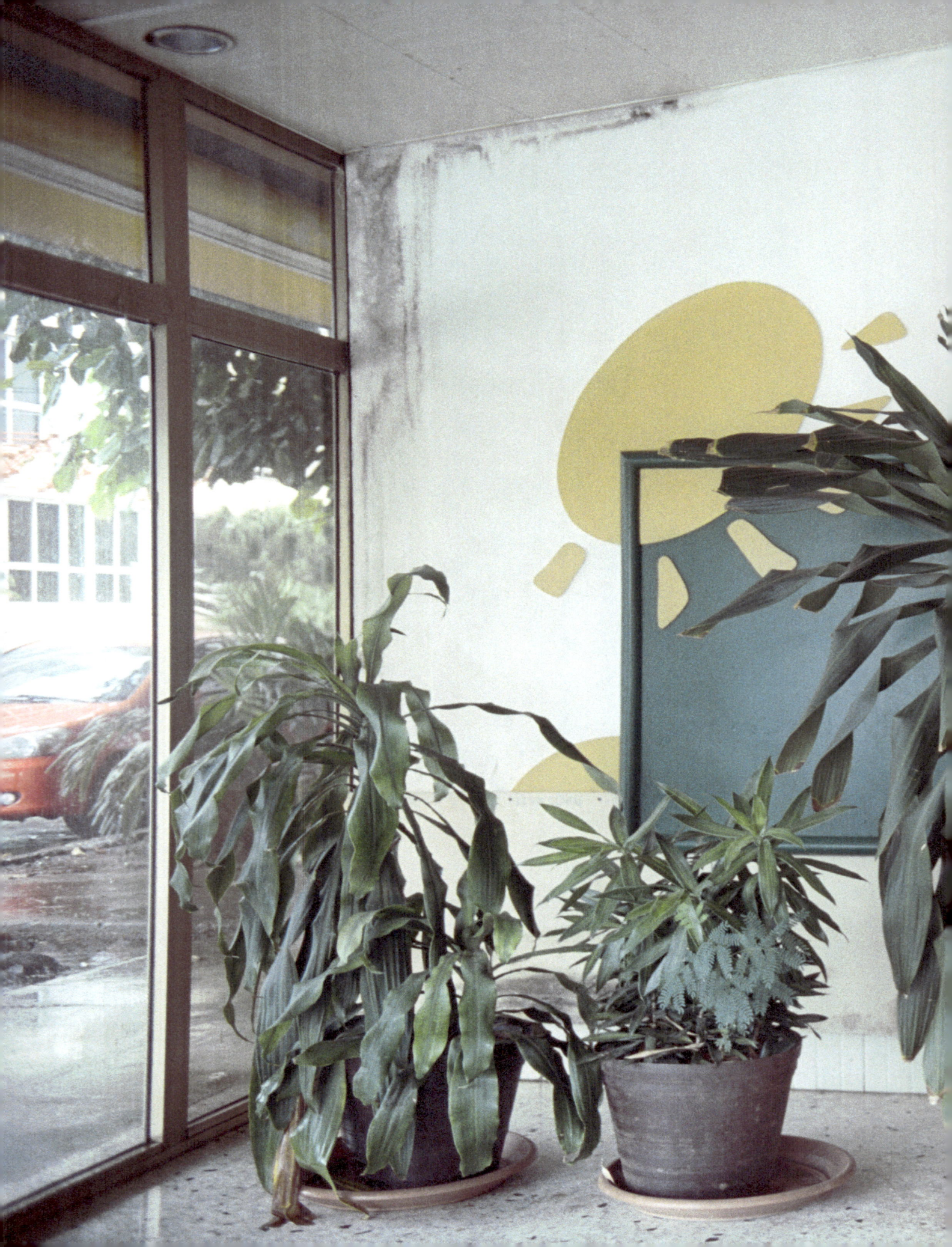

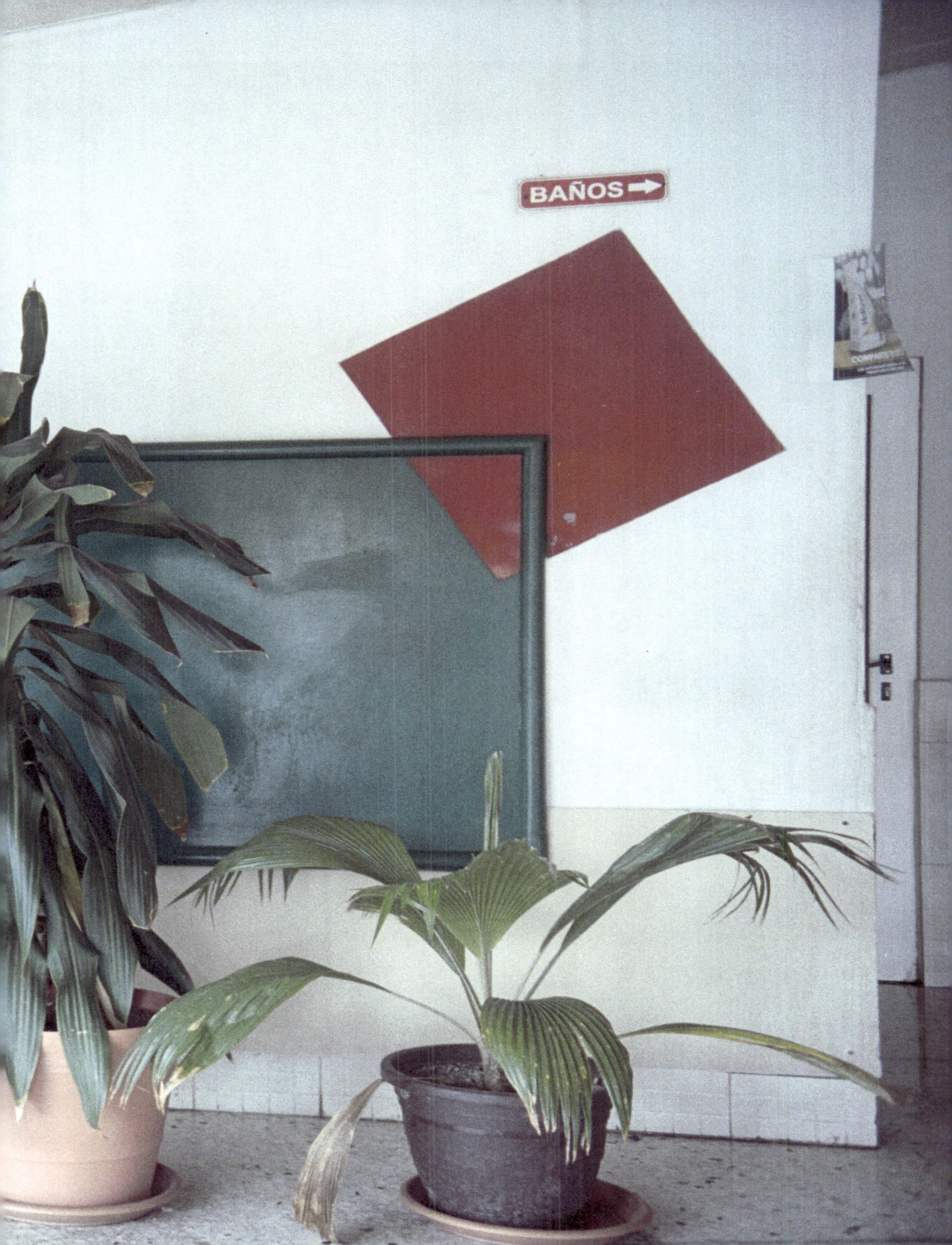

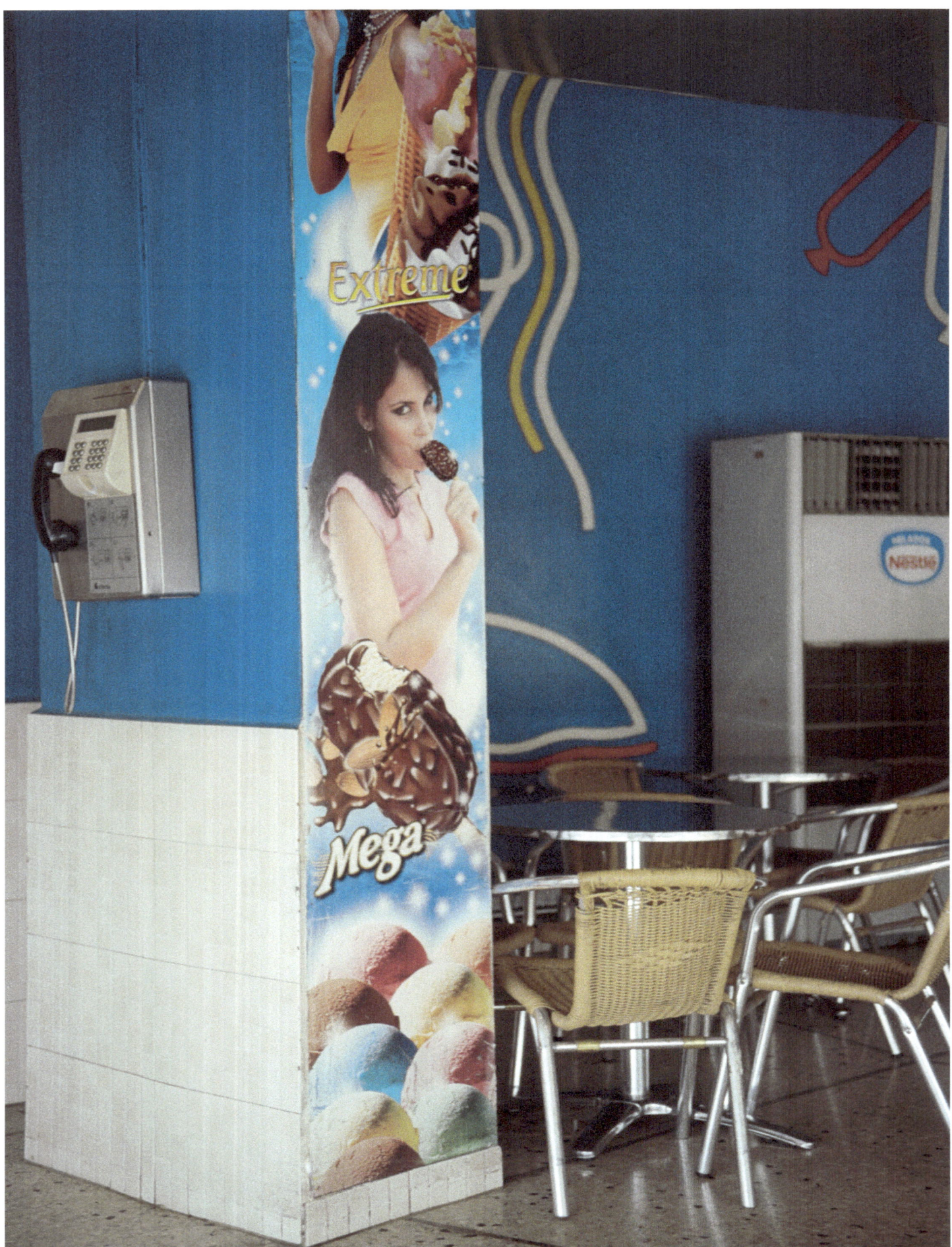

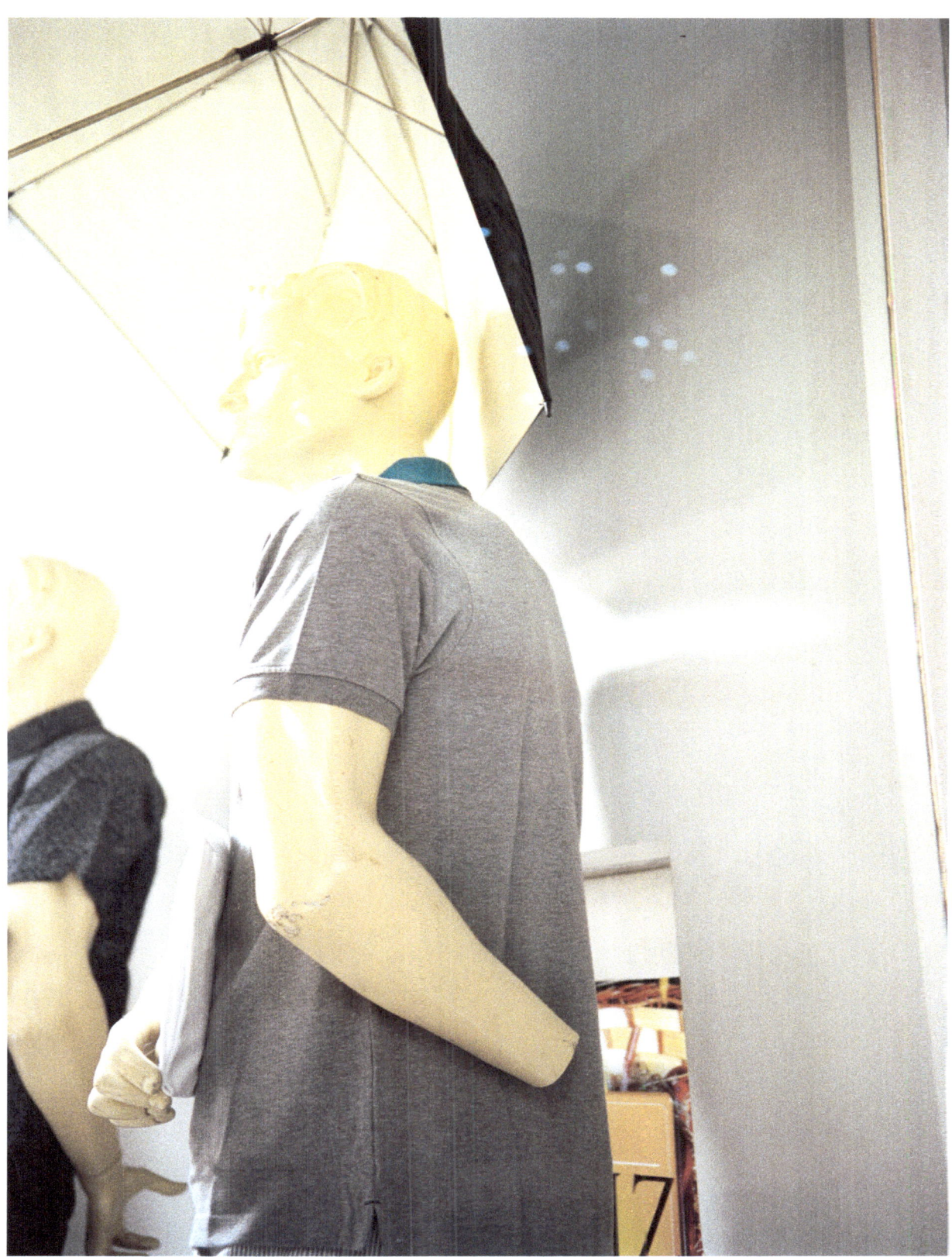

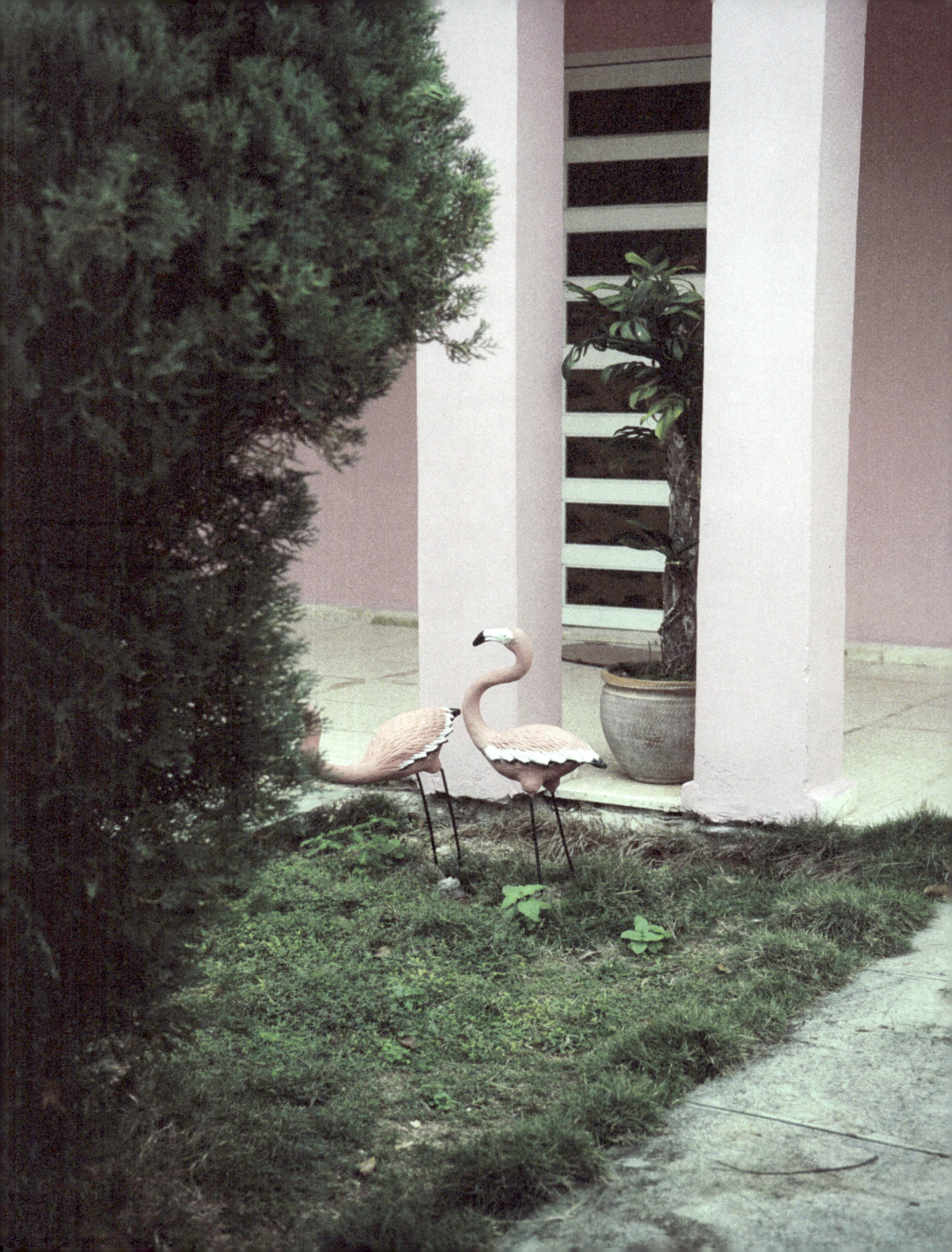

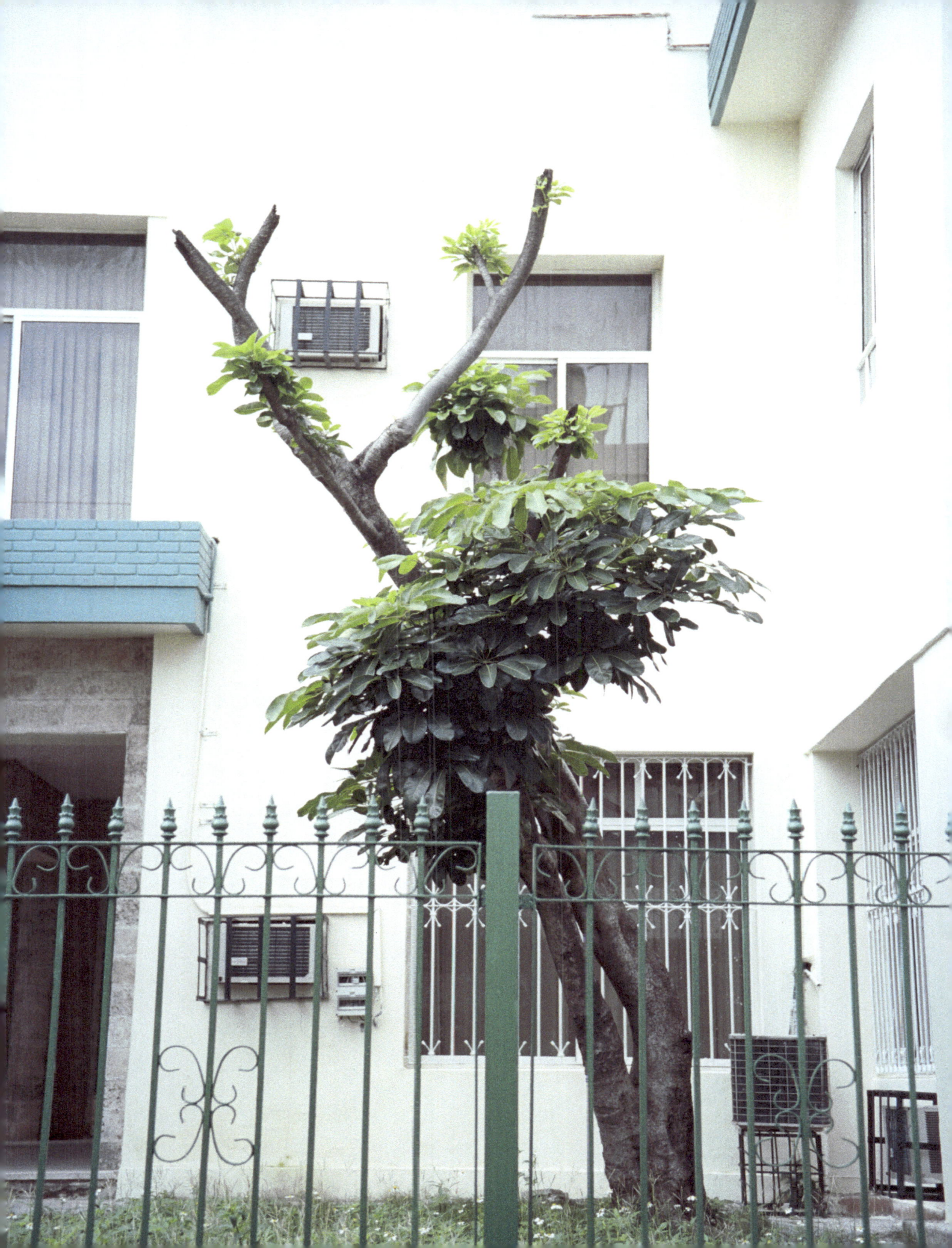

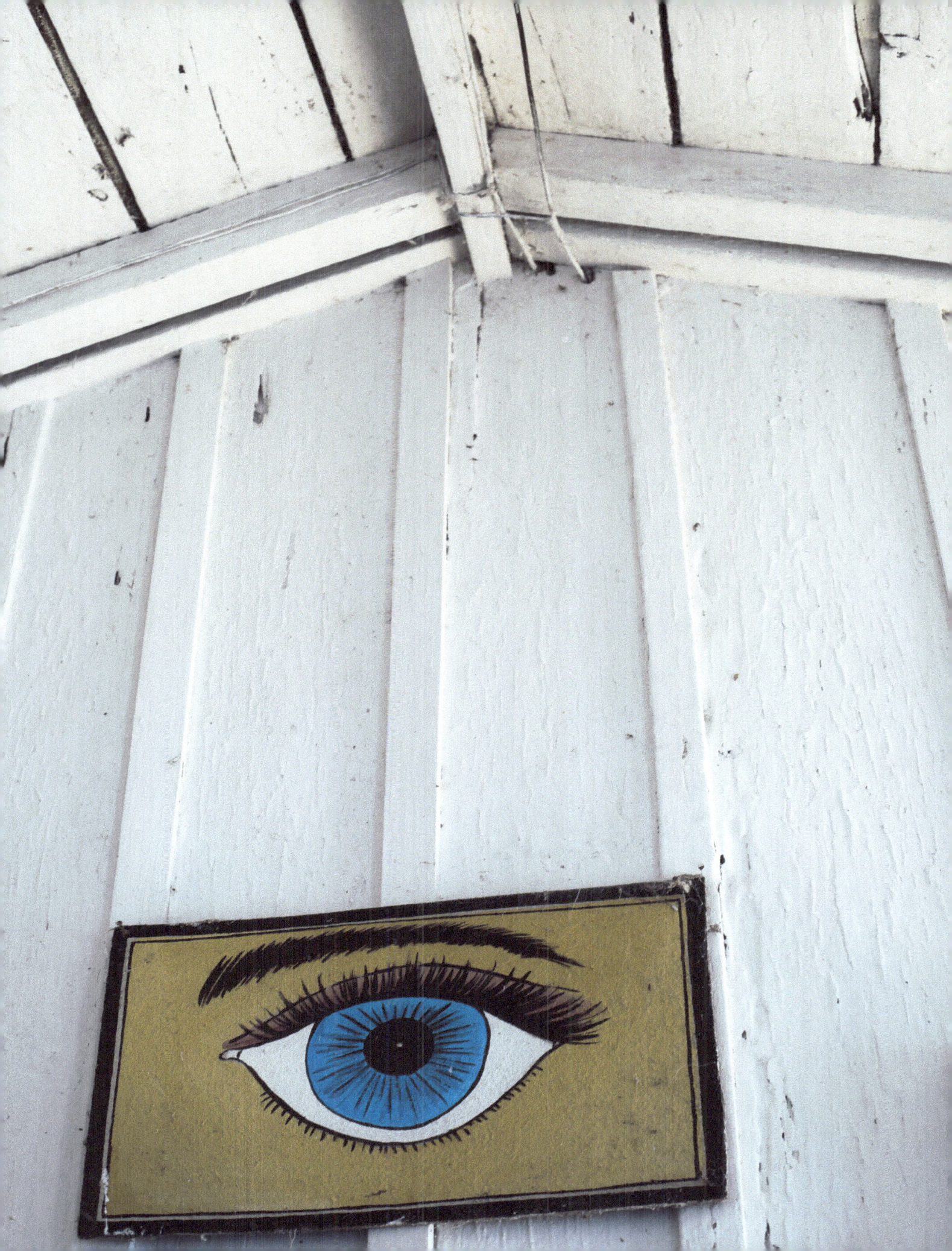